AF595573

YOURS FOREVER

YOURS FOREVER

Shakti Dabas

Notion Press

Old No. 38, New No. 6

McNichols Road, Chetpet

Chennai - 600 031

First Published by Notion Press 2016

ISBN 978-93-5206-741-1

Dedication

This book is dedicated to a genuine friend
who inspired a poet in me.

A result of your trust in the time of despair,
hence Yours Forever it will be.

CONTENTS

PART-I: LOVE

PART-II: RELATIONS

PART-III: SOCIAL ISSUES

PART-I

LOVE

Expressing Love

I never expressed myself; neither did I share my feelings with you
But somewhere, I feel incomplete without you, yes it's true, I do like you
I also know that I really don't show
But I also do think that this you already know
When I see of you, I believe I have not seen anyone like you before
Somehow then I realize, am making myself to look at you more
I know there is no cure, but who told you I am not feeling good
Perhaps it's the best time of my end, when I know I should
It's only me, who is dying
It's only me who is crying
What if she feels for me one day? When am not sure of life, even today
I'll die the sweetest death, wanting you in every breath

Am weak, too weak, but I'll try to hang on for a bit more just to say a little *hi* to you

That's what I have dreamt off for years now but could hardly do

Am leaving you for now my princess, just remember me I was there

I was only made for you my love, but I guess… not here

Vital Loss

I need no one to know am here
I need no one to know I care
I need not to be going to, you went where
I may end up with you down there
I slip on to my daily dose of thoughts
To all what I teach and to all what I was taught
I feel a gap in all the points I bought
Why at all we loved and why at all we fought
It was a premeditated course we took
Right from the first *hi*, the hands we shook
We never wanted it to happen in the first place
Ours was a different tie, a secret case
But we couldn't have continued without a bond for such long
Or else, how could we share such things like our favorite songs
Wouldn't be wrong if I say we were destined to meet
We were caring buddies, what if we couldn't socially greet

Sometimes I do miss that smile of yours
Like a morning dew on a lovely rose
And at times it's painful too, when we just sit across
No words ever spoken, a sudden sense of vital loss

Evolution of Lies

Sometimes I used to think, what I think I thought
And all the texts, the welcome notes and the mention not
The light of your face, your innocence and grace and those twinkling eyes
Your genuine relation, our very own nation, were your sweetest lies
The love and affection, those stories of perfection
The sharing of secrets, those friendly suggestions
Me texting the rhymes, you praising the phrase
The evolution of lies, kind of hard to erase
This made me believe, what I believed I believe wasn't really true
You were just acting around, kind of making some sound, but you weren't in it through
But I am puzzled at the fact, why was I still taking it
Even when I feared in my heart, that you were doing nothing but just faking it

Am Sorry

Am sorry for hurting you
By doing or meaning whatever I did or meant
It was never my aim
It wasn't what I ever intent
Take good care of yourself princess
Coz I won't be there to do that for you
Could have tried to talk a little
But never came up, that's true
Just forgive me for your good
Then forget me for the best
I chose to hate you a little
But it comes out I love you the rest

Hidden Glances

Exchanging pens, then sharing hidden glances
Waiting to talk but ain't ready to take our chances
I want to talk but am afraid I won't
Coz the risk involved comes to haunt
There's always a tension around us, you see
That's why we haven't talked pretty well, you and me
Am in a dilemma and it gets worse when I think
How about we discover an island before I sink
You understand I have an urge
Somehow or the other it finds its way to emerge
You are in the college I know, and there aren't too many lectures today
Can we try and clear our brain, sweet lady what do you say?

Just There

I felt I was sorry for things that I have done
But it's good that I have lost it, rather I had won
I put it on the surface for that you shall care
I made a big blunder, I do that all rare
I wish no one else suffers, with what I have been through
I made a fool of myself; hope the next is not you
My girl was no different, she loved me so much
It was worth dying, the way she made touch
But sooner this feeling goes up in air
And when I got drowning, she felt me just there

Hundred Songs

I would have written you hundred songs
And every written thought would be a mile's long
Now that I am thinking what the words might be
I don't think they'll ever match your ecstasy
I could really read you what you really want
And I don't have a reason, why the hell I can't
Make you crazy… oh baby
Little daisy? Oh may be

A Pound or a Dime

What if that I like you
Do I have to like it too that whatever you do
Or should I be that someone waiting for you
Even when you don't want me to
I might love you a little
But sure that doesn't mean I like you all the time
Sometimes you are too much for a pound
And sometimes you are not even worth a dime

Glittering Eye

I'd like to remember my past again
Not out of a sudden but in the pain
The pain in me of carrying you
All over my face, it's not me but you
I want us back, so don't ever let us go
I've feelings for you that even I don't know
I'll be your villain if not hero to you
You won't understand it's my way of being with you
What's bothering you is kind of hard to get
Don't know about you but it's making me fret
Don't deprive me of the pleasure of your lonely thought that I think
If you want to get into with someone, do it someday after I sink
I really don't know what lies in sky
But I need you more, my *glittering eye*
I live in pieces, quite a few
I may not prove, but the major's you

That Lecture

The words may still be few
As compared to my love for you
No words, no line, not even the delicacy of the sweetest wine
Could be better off you, you are like finest pearl, cutest dew
If life could be re-written, I'll write all you
Though I may, but I want no new
My life was simple but not from now
After you wore those specs, in that lecture of C.A.O

Soul Mate

Like the brightest light in the darkest night
There comes your smile in between our fight
The love you shower and the bless you sprinkle
Will make me love your face even with wrinkle
I wouldn't ask my god for more
When hand in hand we walk the shore
You look so pretty, the charm you had
Could make anyone, anyone go mad
I saw new world, new life with you
So sweet, afresh; just like dew
I want my girl to have your fame
And smile of yours with just my name
I want to live my life with you
And make you smile and smile with you
To woo your dad I'll change my name
To make you mine I'll take the blame

I'll shed my blood but won't see your pain
I'll do my best to break the chain
No crime I have done, No law I broke
Nor Allah told me to choke
Love is bigger than all Gods combined
It's the soul that matches, not just the frame of mind

Soul in My Rhymes

The thought of you that I often thought
Was somehow more real than the real you I ever sought
More often than not
We tend to fight when I choose to not
This is a sudden flow of emotion I perceive
I have given in a lot more than I ever did receive
Looking at you, makes me wonder of my fate
Would I be getting you, be better late
Change is the course of the mother Earth
Likewise, we too, shape out different from birth
What's amazing is the way you see me now
May be it's a dream of mine but I wonder how
I wasn't sure of it, if it really was you
Coz you looked so real, like infant dew
This is the best of you I have seen in the recent times
The one, whose soul is in all my rhymes

Life Without You

I do not belong in here
Not here, not there, not anywhere
It wasn't supposed to turn out this way
I ain't mad, I just didn't have a say
Am not depressed at world, am depressed with my soul
In inner being, I sense a hole
Few laughs do make it good
But with time I realized it makes me sick
It makes me weak, gives me anger
Am becoming dead very quick
What has happened has happened
But shouldn't have happened this way
What if you had talked a bit more?
What if I had cared to stay?
You gave me space, you had me freeze
You block my gaze, you got me breeze
You taught me life, you preach few things
You cut me lose, you gave me wings
When you held my hand and showed you cared

We were genuine in things, we ever shared
But without you, just a few seconds apart, I began to choke
And this life sucks even more, at every corner, at every block
I am an adamant soul my love
I may say I live life and take whatever it gives
But the truth is, there is no life
In this bloody life without you that I live

Last Words

Consider these my words to be the very last
For I know I have done mistakes in past
I don't like me putting up my weakest side
But, like others, I too have lied
In all my lies you may search the data
Nothing means am persona-non-grata
Yes, I lied to you on your face
But I never cheated you in any case
I lied to you I was fine when I was not
I lied to you I didn't shed, when I cried a lot
I lied to you when I said I hate you
Coz it was just the other day I planned to date you
I lied to you *I liked Jane*
I know it was not a good joke, I was kind of insane
But you know what, you lied to me too
You lied to me that day when you proclaimed

We are just good friends and nothing more
Coz I saw in your eyes, they were sore
You lied to me and yourself too
When you said you don't love me
I know you were giving me my way
You were trying to save me
I know I have been a pain and good for none
But I am deeply sorry all what I have done
Oh dear, these words are my last but let me say
I loved only you and will love you even more, each and every day
What say..??

Rediscovering Us

Sometimes I wonder if I was not *I*
And being the other someone of me, would you still be talking to this *I*
Or you knew a bit of me within you
And you didn't wait for things that I told you
Do you just know of me the way I have told?
Or is it that our story on itself unfold
Are you in for me, the way I am into you?
Or you already knew of me deep inside you
Much before we both were through
Would you be still holding my hand, if I were not the way I am to you?
Or would you have lonely made your own start, afresh; a new
Oh sweet lord, with all your burning fire
Let me be molded into a man of her dream; desire
Do not let me know of the truth, if it'll break my heart
Coz someone precious is in it, my lovely sweetheart

Let me be confined in my dream till death
Let me be allowed of love in my every breath
Hope is a thing, may be the best of things, so I hope of you
And if am without my rhymes, with all the crimes, my chances are few
I would like to be accepted of the way I am, so I could be of your way to you
By only then we can start, afresh; anew…

Revenge Time

I was in love with her smile for sometime then
And that sometime I only cherish
I couldn't stand her giggles now
Her laughter is what that makes me perish
The affection I had for her then
I wish I could never have that pain
I loved you once with my soul
I could never love you like that again
Forgetting and forgiving are things of past
I just do not want to repeat just same
I want to make it good, and make new start
I'll do it with someone with your name

I Know You Are Listening

You know I hate fighting you
But I always end up fighting
You Know I don't write to you
But I always keep on trying
You know I have been, kind of liking you
And I think of you a lot
You know I have always been saying it
Don't say you never listen not

No Lies

I too sometimes do
What I hate doing, still I do
Yet, I do not want to repeat
But am uncertain of any unlikely cheat
You my girl, that's all I want
But looking at things, I know I can't
Whatever it takes to make you mine
I'll do it your way, am all fine
Waiting seems a fruitless bid
How hard I try, am just a kid
What more could I possibly do
Should I come and speak up a word or two
These feelings I presume are not felt with word
It's more a communique of eyes, I heard
That means I chat with you the most
Coz often in your eyes, I get lost
What strange bond is binding us I don't know?
I carry you with me, to places I go
If ever you were to say to me, just look me in my eyes
I'll read your heart out, I promise, am telling no lies

ACHILLES

You gave me peace in a lifetime of war
You let a drowning man reach to shore
I owe you the truth you've shown to me
My life, myself, the inner me
No reason has ever been so strong before
To make me go search the heaven's door
I crushed my rivals and earned the sin
But never had I fought the man within
I fought with legends and legends I kill
I've conquered the world but don't know still
What makes me pick my handsome sword?
Why don't I bow to mighty lords?
Am tired of fighting the battle of kings
For now am in love and would love to sing
I'll be a man without any dagger or sword
Like rest of Greeks I'll pray to Gods
I'll take you away to a land of peace
Just you and me on an island of Greece
I got my world I found in you

Just you and me is all I knew
I wanted to live my life with you
And make you smile and smile with you
The princess of Troy, Briseis, my Queen
It's a burning hell you've never seen
But don't you worry just wait for me
I'll come for you like you came for me
To hold your hand I dropped my sword
For once did stumble the mighty lords
The nemesis of Zeus is now on his knees
The victor of war, for love he pleads
I am a man without my name thereon
Am not the same for which I was known
For few moments I thought I deserved you a lot
The cruelest in mind, am harshest not kind
I'd wish more life to die for you
Please show me no tears, I'd cry for you
Am dying out of your love Briseis, not from any arrow or sword
But I'll save Hector's boy, the prince of Troy, I swear on mighty lords
For I'll be most happy in hell to see you smile, then in any heaven to see you ever weep
My love for you is deeper than any ocean, be the depth of the see any deep

PART-II

RELATIONS

Mother

She feeds you with her blood without even seeing your face
She bears your pain with smile and grace
She brings you to Earth risking her life
She gives you birth and give you life
She feels your world and all your needs
She quenches your thirst, with body she feeds
She makes you stand but you walk away
She shows you path but you choose your way
She makes you a man and live your life
But you shows no mercy and walks with wife
Not that she was too old at sixty
But maybe I was too young and extra witty
Life has been so harsh so cruel at her
I should have understood her world, give her strength and be with her
I loved her warmth and her so much
I cared for her but couldn't talk so much
We were poles apart on all matters on Earth
We could never be so close after she gave me birth

It's not that I don't want to be right but I just don't know who to blame

What went so wrong I can't really explain

She lives with me but I lost her touch

I lost her faith could have done so much

But am happy she still see her child

And gives her best to tame my wild

We don't talk that much and stay in mum

But long live my godly figure of mum

It's like the God's with me and I can see her face

A couple of wrinkle with plenty of grace

Like a burning candle in a holy place

So is the beauty of my mother's face

JOURNEY

I make my way of unbeaten track
I travel alone with no look back
Death's an end, but not for men of steel
It's just another passage to cross with guts and zeal
Beyond new edges, beyond new seas
I'll show you my world, oh common please
Living isn't important, important is the way how you die
Smiling isn't important, important are the reasons; which makes you cry
Follow your dreams, for these dreams are yours
Love your soul, even in your household chores
Mine is a story I would like to sing
Ain't got no states but I am my own king
Isn't it great to choose what you really feel?
What if you got any problem, *no big deal*
My name as of now is my own creation
Though I too started off with little appreciation
A little dark with more than a little complication
But now, my journey is my only destination

Worthless Trends

Tragic moments or seconds of bliss
They are larger than life or death, and this
Is a stark reality of things that tend to last on soul
Be it you be any younger or how may you be old
The story goes on again and hardly is it strange
No matter who ever go, no matter which character change
Time is a soothing element that makes you forget the hardest of pain
It makes you better again and soon you enjoy the rain
And then, you do not fear the fear in you
And there dries the stream of tears in you
No more is the feeling of being lost on ways
More likely is the possibility of being lost in our own haze
So dramatically the drama concludes in worthless trends
With all your wealth and earnings proving worthless in end

INNER VOICE

There is something which is getting on to me now
I don't know when it started, I really don't know how
But it seems am running all through a way
I don't know where it's heading, I really can't say
I jump on to the track and catch up the pace
But sooner it fades without much a trace
Do I see what I see and what's happening around
Or, do I say what I say or just making a sound
What's moving is moving and will forever be around
But what's lost is lost, it could never be found
I lost no man, not even girl for a fact
I couldn't sue him even, we didn't have a pact
It's just I do not talk to myself, no more, not in any way
I do have few words sometimes but I just can't say
Am running all around, kind of searching for my sound
And it really trips me out when it's nowhere to be found
They say I am a weirdo and I do not need to do this
But I choke when I say, you need to see this

A Pair of Jeans

I am a simple being, I am a local guy
I have a common dream and think of getting by
I try not to hurt, I try not to fail
I sit and write for purpose and not for telling tale
I have often been a selfish and thought of all my own
I love to be single and walk the road alone
I seldom care for others, for no one cares for me
In writing yes they like but not in front of me
I have never liked to follow the thing that has always been
I search and walk on path, often left unseen
I may be going wrong, may be am too keen; but
If it isn't the work of us, then what's the way of teens?
I live a tougher life, so harder be my pain; yet
I have learned to smile; now smile is in my veins
I wear a mask on myself, as it saves my inner being
My face is for some people, for some the heart is thing
I try and sit with people from whom I could really gain
A word or two of wisdom to help me in the rain

To live a life as mine will numb your little brain
And with little one you are left, your life is all about vain
I take it as it gets, I never do complain
If ever I had to cry, I do that in the rain
I have been as strong as ever I could have
I have worked all on my own and I think that's not too bad
I could have been a sadist but am glad I have never been
I am a happy simple man with single pair of jeans

Again

I, again…
Wanna wanna be the same
Like as always in the pain
Don't know wanna see the rain
Think…
Life has always been a game
Still got nothing of my aim
But do wanna make a name
Cry…
Ain't got nothing much to cry
But I really don't know why
Deep down somewhere yes I cry
Really much…
Wanna wanna make you touch
Nothing nothing bad as such
Just got a heart, nothing much

PART-III

SOCIAL ISSUES

WHY?

I don't know what exactly I am doing on what needs to be done

I am just playing my part in this and I hope it is fun

No one knows why we fall in love

Why don't we stand or rise above

If it is a feeling so cute

So why do they try to cheat or look to shoot

Why is it that some things that we say are not meant to be said

But with all the pain some are left unsaid

Some like to run and chase the goose

While some just sit and share the booze

The vows we took, why they were not kept

In hours of need, why don't we act

On seeing an orphan, why don't we cry

To stop a crime, why don't we try

Why tear of others, don't make us feel

Why a death in a womb, is no big deal

Your dinner's waste, is a meal for two

Where tigers have gone from all the zoos

Why is it one thing have two meanings for two
What's dieting for me, can be starving to you
Why the world we saw in the books around
Was nowhere to be seen on an absurd ground
Why the roses of heaven don't have that smell
Why the followers of *Mao* are beaten like hell
Why the system of ours is not the same as it's written
Why the voters of the land are all tamed and beaten
How a mighty manages to escape the jail
And all of sudden he heads the rail
Why a rapist in real is a hero in reel
Or an award is sold to earn the meal

New Born Cry

When I opened my eyes, I could not find you mom
I was alone in bed and I could feel the storm
I was hoping for love, but not what I was shown
I needed your warmth but I heard you were gone
I cried and wept and thought and slept
What lies ahead and what all is kept
I was abandoned for a thing I never actually did
Oh mom, oh dad, I was just a kid
What makes it worse that you helped my dad
Who's a big sick bastard, who hopes for a lad
My fate would have been something else, if only you were a little strong
I could have also lived, or danced on your song
But you ruined your love, you made that night
And what I would want to ask you now
Did you really made the real love that night?
Weren't you just compromising with life?
And if you don't think so, let me remind you mom
That you are acting like a maid, and not his wife

WHY NOT WINGS TO FLY

God only knows it why
Why only feet for men and not wings to fly
Either we don't deserve the view
Or we lack some things, more than few
Now from out of this few
I presume I know things or two
To know our creator's mind
We got to actually know who is the real creator
Who gave you real birth
Who showed you real path, the real Earth
Who gave you love, you were longing for life
Didn't you feel great in the lap of your wife?
Speak up your heart when you hold your child
Let your eye's cry out in joy and your feeling get wild
That's what we are supposed to do but ain't doing it, right?
Something's got to be wrong in this or we would have been on a flight
I know the power of creation lies in heavenly abode
But the keys to love lay with a woman, the Earthly God

VALLEY

My father was dead by the time I was eight
My mother did tell me then, *Rubina, it's all in fate*
I believed my mother; I believed that's how it is
But Bashir was different, didn't buy a point of this
For he had seen him die, for he too wanted to cry
But not a drop he felt, no matter what he tried
He saw his father pleading for life
The swearing on kids, the swearing on wife
He did tell me then, *They didn't listen once and shot in twice*
I swear on god, they weren't any nice…
That day what I heard from him, I could not dismiss as a lie
He was full of anger; just hatred was all in his eye
Poor mother suffered another shock when he crossed the valley
Cried a river, felt a sigh, looked at sheets, but couldn't tally
Days, months and years passed but he couldn't be found or traced

Another month, another year and all those memories were erased

Then one day, those not so nice men took our neighbor's son away

The last I saw of him he was out to play

And then we heard uproar down the street

The mass carrying a young body and I could only see his feet

The neighbor's son didn't have his father by him

Or he would have saved his son's life, and the dead today won't be him

I believed my mother that day when she told me *it's all in fate*

But cannot accept it now, not now this late

Now I wonder what Bashir did, wasn't that wrong

May be he was weak and wasn't that strong

But this certainly you shouldn't call Jihad, it's just a fight

Our struggle for freedom, our fight for rights

Mao Mind

Born in grass, brought up in shades
What life I had prior to raids
Just nature I loved, I owned no land
With sweat I had ploughed barren land
It's what I am born with, it's what I have
It's all am left with, that's all I ever had
For years we have lived here, how cold they want us to flee
It's about all of us, not one or just me
Don't brand me a rebel, don't mark any line
For home everyone fights, like me at nine
We are no Maoists, but put up in error
We are victims of fate and state run terror
We are abused by men, we voted to chair
We are blamed by men, who knows nothing of here
Our life's been a story of struggle, we'll fight till end
We did no wrong and we will not bend
We don't kill for fun, we kill to protest
In a billion's world, it's the toughest test
We are no cowards, who make women go upfront

We fight in toto, as we all have borne the brunt
I use more of *we*, coz it's not just the voice of one
I carry the heart of all dead, but none
Noticed my pain until they not see my arm
They want us go back now and plough the farm
For am happy to go back and live on my land
But I see no world, I see no land
For our mother was sold to corporate, with greasing hands
So, I carry my struggle, my fight for land

A Wait Forever

I am waiting for men to say what they mean
I am waiting for actions on paper to be seen
I am waiting for end of the battle for land
I am waiting for someone to offer a hand
I am waiting for a mom to fight for her child
I am waiting for tigers to return to the wild
I am waiting for hatred to come to an end
I am waiting for leaders to act what they meant
I am waiting for pundits to return to their lives
I am waiting for soldiers to return to their wives
I am waiting for riots to come to a halt
I am waiting for someone to admit to their fault
I am waiting for my dad to call me a name
I am waiting for my life to be just same

www.ingramcontent.com/pod-product-compliance
Lightning Source LLC
LaVergne TN
LVHW090317160826
845684LV00001B/5